TODAY'S F

Book 5 – The Fivefold Office Series

COLETTE TOACH

AMI BOOKSHOP

www.ami-bookshop.com

Today's Prophet
Book 5 – The Fivefold Office Series

ISBN-10: 1626640351
ISBN-13: 978-1-62664-035-1

1st Printing June 2018

Published by **Apostolic Movement International, LLC**
E-mail Address: admin@ami-bookshop.com
Web Address: www.ami-bookshop.com

Contents

THE OLD TESTAMENT PROPHET DEFINITION

Chapter 01 – The Old Testament Prophet Definition

One of the first things you learn as a parent is that you should not give your children candy first thing in the morning. It is a universal parenting rule, and we know why we give those rules as parents.

Between the sugar and the coloring, it is not going to be a good day for them, or for you. They may like that candy and try to sneak that candy, but you and I both know that it is not a good idea to consume that many Skittles or M&Ms first thing in the morning for breakfast.

All that sugar is going to give them a tummy ache. Then, the next thing you know, mom is mopping up the floor. Mom needs to clean up and chase after the kid who is on a sugar rush.

It goes without saying that if you even consider yourself as a mediocre parent, you know that you do not start your child's day off with M&Ms. Unfortunately, in the Church, we have not seemed to get this message yet.

There is so much emphasis on the candy, that we have given the Church a tummy ache. This is even more valid when we speak about the prophetic ministry.

There has been so much hype on prophecies, visions, revelations, and all the signs and wonders and fantastic stuff. It is like giving the Church candy without giving them a meal first.

We have prophets running around and handing the candy out, and there is nothing wrong with some candy. I do not withhold candy from my children all the time. Yet, there is a time and a place for it.

If you know anything about this ministry, you will realize that we are trying to bring balance in the prophetic ministry. That is certainly the core of this book, to bring balance.

When I bring this balance, even you prophets who enjoy the candy are going to feel a peace. Even though candy tastes nice, even you get sick of it sometimes.

If that were all you ever ate, you would get a cavity in your tooth at the very least. You would also get a tummy ache and start craving vegetables and meat. None of us can live off candy.

Time to Move on to Maturity

Many of you that have a prophetic calling know that there has to be something more. You know that there has to be something deeper.

You think, "Surely, the reason why I die so much and why I have had to pay such a price is proof that being in this office has got to be something more than what I see.

Is this it for the Church? Is what we are seeing right now all that there is for prophetic ministry?"

No. There is a whole new level of prophetic office that God is maturing in His saints right now. He is maturing this in you. It is time that you move on to that prophetic maturity.

> **Everyone knows that a prophet is a person that prophesies, right?**

> **WRONG!**

If you are one that has always prophesied and known that you have a prophetic call on your life, you share your visions, prophecies, and dreams. But then, you get to a point in your call where you say, "Lord, is that it?"

You get to church where people are waiting for the next great revelation, and now you have to try to get something that is a little more profound than the week before.

So now, you have to "up" the prophecy magnitude. You have to prophesy more to more people and more often. Otherwise, you are going to start losing popularity and feeling that you are not fulfilling your call.

You wear yourself out prophesying here and there and sharing your visions, and since the prophetic is so high in the church right now, the pastor is happy to bring you along.

He says, "You stand here and prophesy. That is your place."

I do not know about you, but I do not like being labeled.

"That is who you are. You are the person that prophesies."

"You are the singer. That is who you are."

"You are just the dream lady. That is who you are."

Perhaps deep inside you are saying to yourself, "I am so much more than a mouthpiece or someone that gets visions. Do you not see me? I am a person. I have a mandate and a call. I do not know what it is yet, but somewhere underneath all of this prophesying lies a prophet that is dying to come out."

This is your "coming out" moment. This book is a message to you to let you know that it is time for the prophet in you to come out.

The Old Testament Prophet Defined

> **Numbers 11:29** *Then Moses said to him, "Are you zealous for my sake? Oh, that all the Lord's*

people were prophets, and that the LORD would put His Spirit upon them!"

Moses understood the pressure of being the only one that could hear from God and give the word of God.

So God anointed leaders of tens, hundreds, and thousands. Moses held a gathering and the Spirit of God fell on those leaders, and they started to prophesy. Two of them were in the camp prophesying and Moses was asked, "Should we stop them?"

He said, "Please don't. I wish everybody could be a prophet and everyone could hear from God. It would make my job a lot easier."

Moses actually liked the law a little bit more. I can imagine having to give the prophetic words all the time became quite tiresome for him. Yet, in the Old Testament there were very specific people that God called to be prophets.

Defining the O.T. Prophet

Not just anybody could be a prophet. It was very clear when God called a prophet because they were the only ones that prophesied. He would pick select individuals who had quite the life.

They had a life of separation and holiness. The Spirit would come upon them. They were very special.

When you start looking at the word "prophet" in the Old Testament and what it means in the New

Testament, you start seeing a very clear distinction beginning to take place.

This distinction has not been made clear in the body of Christ. So, we have a lot of confusion and immaturity because the prophet is seen simply as, "one who prophesies".

Nobody digs deeper to go further with their calling. They stop at the gift of prophecy. Yet, they are always feeling like there is something missing. There is something that they are not quite getting a hold of.

This is what I want you to get a hold of in this book. Let's look at the nabiy' prophet. Do you know what that is? That is actually the word for prophet in the Old Testament.

Here is the Strong's definition:

> 5030
>
> nabiy' {naw-bee'}
>
> AV - prophet 312, prophecy 1, them that prophesy 1, prophet
>
> 1) spokesman, speaker, prophet
>
> 1a) prophet
>
> 1b) false prophet
>
> 1c) heathen prophet

In Other Words...

Let me see if I can break down exactly what a prophet was in the Old Testament.

> *1 Samuel 10:11 And it happened, when all who knew him formerly saw that he indeed prophesied among the prophets, that the people said one to another, "What is this that has come upon the son of Kish? Is Saul also among the prophets?"*

Now, we know that Saul was not a prophet. He was far from it. However, back then when he started prophesying, lying down, and doing crazy things, they thought, "Is Saul among the prophets now?"

> *1 Kings 18:22 Then Elijah said to the people, "I alone am left a prophet of the LORD; but Baal's prophets are four hundred and fifty men."*

That is kind of weird. God was not the only one who had prophets, but the heathen gods had prophets too. Baal had prophets of his own that prophesied. Confused yet?

So... what is a prophet exactly?

It is very simple. In the Old Testament, if someone prophesied, they were a prophet. Whether they were a heathen or an Israelite - they were considered to be a prophet. It all depended on the fact that a spirit came upon them and that they spoke on behalf of that god.

In our case, the prophets of God spoke the thoughts of Yahweh. The prophets of Baal spoke the thoughts of Baal. It is very simple.

> **For those who lived in the Old Testament era, the distinction was pretty obvious. A spirit would come upon them, and they would speak. In other words, the gods could not speak for themselves, so they needed a spokesman to relay messages to people.**

That is why Moses was called a prophet as well as Jeremiah and even John the Baptist. Why were they called prophets? It is because they spoke on behalf of God. Nice and simple.

What We Have Today

There was a very clear way that God spoke to people in the Old Testament. By the end of this book, you are really going to understand the difference between the Old and New Testament and what an incredible inheritance we have today.

Before Christ, they did not have the option to hear God when they wanted to. In fact, there were sometimes hundreds of years between prophetic words.

Can you imagine not hearing God's voice your entire lifetime, and going only on living by the law? I am talking about the strict letter of the law. They did not even have the New Testament, and for a long season, not even all the prophets had been sent yet.

Sometimes, there were hundreds of years that went by without hearing so much as a whisper from God. So, you can be sure that when there was someone who cropped up that could speak God's voice, it was a big deal.

The Word said that it had been very quiet before Samuel came along. So, when Samuel, suddenly, even as a child, spoke on behalf of God, it was a big deal.

The people thought, "God is speaking to His people again."

They could not hear Him any other way. They had to go by the strict letter of the law and by sheer willpower. So, yes, when someone had the anointing come upon them, and they spoke on behalf of God, they were a prophet.

Whether he prophesied once or one hundred times, he was a prophet because he spoke on behalf of God.

The 3 Ways God spoke in the Old Testament

> *1 Samuel 28:6 And when Saul inquired of the LORD, the LORD did not answer him, either by dreams, or by Urim, or by the prophets.*

There were three ways that God spoke to people in the Old Testament. These three ways were:

1.   Through Dreams
2.   Through Urim and Thummim
3.   Through His Prophets

In each case, it required the Holy Spirit to come upon the person externally and move upon him. After the word was received, the anointing lifted.

Dreams

Why dreams? It is because they were asleep, and they could not resist the word. They were not in a place of sin, so God could descend upon them in that moment and give them a dream.

In fact, that is how Solomon heard the Lord, through dreams. Even David said, "I got this pattern in a vision of the night." Daniel also heard God through dreams.

This is why we see way more dreams in the Old Testament than we do in the New Testament. It is because the Holy Spirit would descend and then leave. He could not remain with sinful man.

If they had performed their sin offering, for that moment, they were righteous. Yet, when they sinned again, they had to do it again, because the blood of Christ had not yet been spilled to redeem them.

For the moment, while they lived in that bubble of holiness... for that little time, the Holy Spirit could come upon sinful man and move.

Yet, the blood of Christ changed all that. Now, when the Father looks upon us, He does not see our sin. He sees us through the blood of Jesus, and we are righteous in His sight.

Whether you have sinned or not, if you are born again, the Father sees the blood. Instead of having to go to the altar every five minutes, we carry that altar in us through the blood of Christ.

That is why the Holy Spirit can dwell with us like He could not in the Old Testament. So that is why those are the only three ways that God could speak in the Old Testament.

He would come upon a prophet, and that is why it was so uncontrollable. With Saul, the Holy Spirit came upon him, and he prophesied.

Now, you and I know that this is not how it happens in the New Testament. You have probably looked at the Old and New Testament and thought, "I see some similarities, but that is not how I prophesy."

God does not have to give me a backhand or throw me to the ground and make me strip myself naked and prophesy. (Thank the Lord for that!)

Brother... if you are being thrown to the ground and stripping naked to prophesy, then you need some deliverance!

There is definitely a distinction between the Old and New Testament prophet, and that is the distinction that I am trying to lead you through.

Urim and Thummim

Then, there is the Urim and Thummim which I have taught about before in *Prophetic Essentials* and *Prophetic Functions*. That is what the high priests had in their ephods, and it was a "yes or no" answer. (Exodus 28:30, 1 Samuel 28:6)

God would lead, and then they would say, "Should I marry this person?"

"Yes."

"Should I move house?"

"No."

It was very simple. There was also God speaking through the prophets. So, if there were no prophets around, there were only Urim and Thummim and dreams.

That is a hard life. You can imagine the stir when John the Baptist came on the scene. It had been hundreds of years since they had heard God speak.

> **They were in captivity, and the last of the prophets that they had heard were before they had been dragged away.**

God seemed so silent. How dramatic that must have been to see John the Baptist coming up from the wilderness speaking the word of God. Everybody recognized the anointing. Can God make an entrance or what?

The Lord was trying to make a very serious point.

"Transition! Change!"

It is almost like He silenced the prophets for those hundreds of years to say, "It is over. The old covenant is over. It is dead."

Then, when He does finally bring another prophet forth, he looks nothing like a typical prophet. He has a completely different ministry.

NEW GIFTS FOR A NEW GENERATION

Chapter 02 – New Gifts for a New Generation

Identifying Today's Prophet

> **Numbers 12:6** Then He said, "Hear now My words: If there is a prophet among you, I, the LORD, make Myself known to him in a vision; I speak to him in a dream.
> 7 Not so with My servant Moses; He is faithful in all My house.
> 8 I speak with him face to face, even plainly, and not in dark sayings; And he sees the form of the LORD. Why then were you not afraid to speak against my servant Moses?"

VERSUS:

On the Day of Pentecost:

> **Acts 2:17** And it shall come to pass in the last days, says God, that I will pour out of My Spirit on all flesh: your sons and your daughters shall prophesy, your young men shall see visions, your old men shall dream dreams.
> 18 And on My menservants and on My maidservants I will pour out My Spirit in those days; and they shall prophesy.

You are already familiar with Numbers 12. It speaks about how, if God wanted to speak, He did so through the prophets.

However, in Acts 2 everything changed. The day of Pentecost came and even the male and female servants could prophesy. What exactly happened there? In this moment, a huge separation was brought between the old and the new.

Behold I do a New Thing…

> *Isaiah 43:19 Behold, I will do a new thing,*
> *Now it shall spring forth;*
> *Shall you not know it?*
> *I will even make a road in the wilderness*
> *And rivers in the desert.*

New Gifts for a New Nation

> *Ephesians 4:8 Therefore He says:*
> *"When He ascended on high,*
> *He led captivity captive,*
> *And gave gifts to men."*
>
> *11 And He Himself gave some to be apostles, some prophets, some evangelists, and some pastors and teachers,*

I want you to look at the part that says, "gave gifts to men".

Tell me something. If the category of prophet that they already knew existed, why did God need to give new gifts to men? Why does it list the prophet as a new gift to be given to men… if it already existed?

Could it be that the reason why the fivefold ministry was listed so specifically was because it was something new? Could it be that it was something that did not exist before?

Otherwise, why would Jesus have said, "I give gifts to men, the apostle, the prophet, the teacher, the pastor, and the evangelist? I give to you these gifts."

Why did He make such a point, if they already existed?

Reason being, they did not already exist. These gifts that God gave to the Church were new gifts. They were gifts that had not existed before.

We can sure see the types and shadows. We know the nature of the Word, the language, the flow, and the pattern. We know how the Lord flows from one revelation to the next.

So, we do see a thread through the Old Testament in types and shadows, but there is no doubt that, on the day of Pentecost, something shattering took place.

We read in the book of Hebrews, chapter 8:13, *In that He says, "A new covenant," He has made the first obsolete. Now what is becoming obsolete and growing old is ready to vanish away.*

Not only did the Lord introduce the gifts of the Spirit and body ministries, but suddenly, we also have apostles and evangelists, which did not exist before! If this is all true, then what makes you think that the prophet as they knew it in the Old Testament would stay the same?

If the evangelist is new, the apostle is new, the way the teacher teaches is new, and who the pastor was is new, do you think that God would change four of them and leave the prophet out?

Can you see how much confusion this has brought to the body of Christ? You have prophets looking at the Old Testament as an example of how they should be acting today.

We need to focus on the New Testament prophet. The prophet that existed in the Old Testament does not exist anymore. As I shared already in *Today's Evangelist*, the Old Testament prophet exists as two offices now: evangelist and prophet.

God did something new. Now, in our New Testament era, not everyone who prophesies is a prophet.

The Lord must have changed that one up when He heard the prayer of Moses.

Moses said, "Oh that everyone would be prophets."

Now Moses was not saying that he wished that everyone would be in the office of prophet. He was saying that he wished that everyone could hear from God for themselves.

He was saying that he wished that everyone could prophesy and be a spokesman, and it was as if the Lord heard that cry of Moses' heart, because He poured His Spirit out on all men.

So now, everyone can prophesy and flow in the gifts of the Spirit.

So, now we have a dilemma. If every believer can prophesy, and you are regarding today's prophet as being the same caliber of the Old Testament Prophet, then you... prophet... are out of a job.

Defining the Prophet

If you believe that one who prophesies is a prophet, you are out of a job because everyone can do it. My thirteen-year-old can prophesy.

When you raise up someone in the kingdom of God and put the Spirit of God in them, the gifts are naturally going to manifest, because the Holy Spirit manifests those gifts where He wills to whom He wills.

You do not have to be super-duper or saved for many years. I have seen someone born again for two days who is able to prophesy.

So, will you say of such a believer, "He is a prophet"?

He has been born again for two days! Are you kidding me?

How much damage has this done to the Church? The Lord gives this gift to someone who, maybe down the road, is called to prophetic ministry, but not necessarily.

They are barely born again, seeing visions and prophesying, and people push them beyond what God intends. They do not even learn to function in any of the body ministries.

Take Time to Age (Mature)

They do not even go through the evangelistic or the pastoral ministries to temper their character and mature them. Is it any surprise that Paul said in 1 Timothy 3 that these are the rules that you need to abide by as an overseer?

"He must not be new (or a novice) in the Lord."

He was not just speaking about pastors, but leaders in the church, the elders. If you look at the New Testament, you will see that the elders all carried different fivefold ministry callings.

Some of them were prophets, some were pastors, and some were apostles. That is why he used the words "elder" and "bishop". He was referring to all of the fivefold ministry.

He said, "Do not appoint someone who is new in the Lord. Do not appoint someone whose house is not in order. Do not appoint someone who goes to wine to meet their need.

You need to appoint someone who has been along the way for a bit and who has the respect of those around him, because this also proves his character. Then, he should have that position."

What damage have we done by seeing someone flowing in the gifts of the Spirit and saying, "That is your calling. That is your ministry"?

What pressure have we put on people to be something that they are not yet ready to be? They have not yet had time to go through the fire and have their characters tempered.

We have done a great disservice to the body of Christ. I pray that together we can bring balance, starting with ourselves and leading that victory to the rest of the body of Christ.

The Birth of a New Kind of Prophet

We see on the day of Pentecost the birth of a new kind of prophet. I would daresay that it is only now, so many years later, that we are starting to see the beginning stages of maturity.

Every now and again you get one that goes against the grain and moves past the "prophecy thing". They say, "I am done with this. Let the baby prophets prophesy."

If you ever come to one of our fivefold ministry leadership meetings, you will notice that I do not do a lot of prophecy up front. Why should I? You can prophesy. What do you need my prophetic words for?

It is different if we have a whole congregation of new converts that really need to hear the Lord. Of course, we will prophesy if that is the case. However, you can hear God for yourself.

Should we prophets not be confirming what you already have heard from God? That is what we do in personal ministry. We confirm what you already know. That is how prophetic maturity operates.

If you need a prophetic word, we will give you a prophetic word. However, that is not the beginning and end of the prophetic ministry.

If you are a true prophet, you are thinking, "Thank you, Jesus."

Prophesying lays such a pressure on you. "If that is your label, and you are not prophesying, then what is wrong with you?"

Caving Under the Pressure

People say, "Did you lose your gift? Did God take your gift away? Maybe you sinned or did something wrong? What is wrong with you?"

Then, you end up going beyond what God intends. You end up prophesying out of your mind. Once you take that step, because of the pressure, you are going to start prophesying a couple of things that are from a spirit alright... but just not from the Holy Spirit.

If you are looking for something, you are going to find it. I have seen so many prophets go astray because of that pressure. They think that they are going to lose their position in church because they cannot prophesy anymore.

Someone comes to you for ministry, and you do not get revelation. You think, "I better get a revelation. I better know how to pray. I better do or say something."

It is not very acceptable to say that God is not speaking.

"You are a prophet, aren't you? Isn't it your gift?"

You are the Gift

Do not get me started on that! Listen to my prophetic teachings. Do not let me hear that come out of your mouth... "my gift".

Just a reminder in case you forgot... You *are* the gift!

God gave gifts to the Church, apostles, prophets, and so on. You put your name there. You are the gift. Let that sink into your head.

The gifts of the Spirit are manifested by whom? Are they called the gifts of Colette Toach?

"I need a word of prophecy."

"Ok. Let me just prophesy to you."

"I need a vision."

"Ok. Let me just get one for you."

Not even an evangelist would get up and share the gospel without the Holy Spirit moving him. Would a teacher teach if he did not have a principle to teach?

He would say, "I am going to wait on God until he gives me something to share."

If a teacher would say that, then why should it be different for the prophet? Why are we expected to prophesy and get revelation because it is "our gift"?

> **No. We are not psychics. We are prophets. It is the Holy Spirit that manifests the gifts as He wills. He may want to manifest the gift of prophecy through a teacher today.**

> **Should we not give Him that liberty? It is His church and all. We are the gift. It is His church. It is not our gift.**

If you want to upset the teacher in me, say that the gifts of revelation are your gifts.

Don't tell me that prophecy is your gift. It is not your gift.

The Holy Spirit manifests that gift when He wants. It is His gift. You are just the vessel. He just pours through you, and it comes out. However, sometimes He does not pour through you.

Does that make you less of a prophet if you do not prophesy? Knowing this takes a bit of the pressure off.

So, here is the big question. If a prophet does not prophesy, what does he do? I have written a library of books on that, but let's see if I can give you a summarized version here. Perhaps as you read through my list, you can think of some of your own revelations that you can add to the comparison.

Comparing Old and New Testament Prophet

Old Testament Functions	New Testament Comparisons
To call Israel back to God	The evangelist calls the world to God. The Church is already IN God!
To bring conviction to the sinful nations (Jonah)	Conviction is the work of the evangelist
To turn from their ways – avoid judgment	Avoiding judgment – work of evangelist as

	well. Salvation is now in faith!
To pass on God's messages	To pass on God's messages – God can speak to every believer now
To give a vision of the future	Still the work of the prophet
To decree things into the earth (To build up and tear down)	Still the work of the prophet
To appoint kings	Still the work of the prophet
Worked alone	Not so in the NT – they all worked in teams

THE IRONY: BROKEN FIXES BROKEN

Chapter 03 – The Irony: Broken Fixes Broken

I want to look at the functions of the Old Testament prophet and how they relate now to the New Testament. Keep in mind that we now have the indwelling of the Holy Spirit and that we have the fivefold ministry as well.

As we go through the functions of the Old Testament prophet, you are going to start seeing a sorting taking place.

Old Versus New Testament Functions

Firstly, in the Old Testament, a prophet called Israel back to God. In the New Testament, the evangelist calls the world to God because the Church is already in God.

How can we call the Church back to God when the Scripture is so clear that we have been written on His heart? He has inscribed us. We are in Him. The minute you were born again, you were made in Him.

Yes, you may have backslidden or done something that you should not have done. Does that suddenly make the blood of Christ evaporate?

Is the blood of Christ so scared of sin, or the bad word that you let out when you slipped in the shower this morning, that it just evaporated?

So now you need a prophet to knock on your door and say, "Turn back to God?"

Really?!

"I have come to call the Church back to God."

Well, I never knew that it was lost. Does God know? You should let Him know. Say, "God – sorry to break the news to you, but your Church left."

This is what happens when you confuse the Old and New Testament. You see the prophet doing that in the Old Testament, and you think, "They spoke to Israel, so we should be speaking to the Church and telling them to return to God."

I am not speaking about someone standing up and igniting the fire for God again. I am not speaking about someone who is speaking to the backslider and saying, "God has forgiven you."

I am talking about those who are standing up and prophesying that the Church is going to hell and that the Church is lost and needs to go back to God. We never lost God.

We may have lost the fire, and we may even be full of sin and need to go through the refining fire to get rid of some of our dross. However, the Holy Spirit is still in us. He did not just take a back door when we did something wrong. He is still there.

I am still in Christ. Why are you turning me back? Set me on fire, but do not turn me back. I never left. He never left. We are still one even though you cannot see it so well.

We just need to get rid of the junk so that you can see it again.

Yet, the evangelist is calling the world to Christ. He is going out there and saying, "World, come to Christ!"

That is why I said that the Old Testament prophet is a split of what we see today in the New Testament of the evangelist and the prophet.

Secondly, the Old Testament prophet was meant to bring conviction to sinful nations. The evangelist brings conviction the most out of the fivefold ministry. Why? It is because he operates with the Holy Spirit.

So, sorry prophets, you just lost another function.

Then, the prophet was to tell others to turn from their ways and avoid the judgment of God. The blood of Christ now saves us from judgment. Yet, we know that when we sin, we sin against ourselves more than anything else.

We open the door for the enemy to attack us. This is again the work of the evangelist, to come and bring conviction of sin.

He says, "You are going down the wrong road, and you are going to hit a wall."

There goes another one of the prophetic functions. Soon, there is going to be nothing left for you, prophets.

Prophets were also meant to pass on God's messages. That was probably the primary function of the prophets in the Old Testament.

They would say, "Thus says the Lord, you must go here or there. God is going to send you to Babylon. You are going to be destroyed. You are going to be torn down. You are going to be built up."

When David wanted to build the temple, a prophet came and said, "God says no, because your hands are full of blood. Your son will build the temple." They relied heavily on the prophets to hear from God.

In the New Testament, every believer can hear from God. Just when we thought that there was something that we could hold onto, it was taken away. Everyone can hear from God. You should know by now, if you have read any of my prophetic books, that it is for the prophet to teach God's people to hear Him for themselves.

> **Everyone can hear from God. That is not solely the function of the prophet anymore. We do not run to the prophet to hear from God any more. We now run to the prophet to learn how to hear from God for ourselves.**

That is what the New Testament prophet looks like. Then, they gave a vision of the future. That is what I love about the prophets.

When the Israelites were living it up, the prophets were prophesying about how much the people were going to die. When the Israelites were dying, the prophets told them that, one day, they were going to live it up.

That is just a prophet for you. That has not changed. That stuck through to the New Testament. Prophets are still full of that.

The prophet also decreed God's plans into the earth. This function is still very much shared between the evangelist and the prophet. It is the evangelist that will cry on his face for a nation and decree salvation to that nation again and again.

The prophet, on the other hand, will be decreeing on behalf of the body of Christ. You would not be the first prophet that God has used in the ministry of intercession.

You have been on your knees saying, "Father, release this anointing on your people. Release that blessing. Open that door. Close that door. Tear that ministry down. Build that ministry up."

This is still very much the realm of the prophet, but it is also shared with the evangelist when it comes to decreeing over nations.

The prophets were also used to appoint kings. This is again another function that the prophets have kept. You are still called of God to appoint kings, and I will tell you why as we continue through this book and start looking at the signs of someone standing in prophetic office.

Another major difference between the Old and New Testament is that in the Old Testament, the prophets worked alone a lot. Only when you see Elijah and Elisha and the sons of the prophets do you see that there was a community.

Yet, for the most part, you see prophets going out on their own. We see Jonah going out on his own and Ezekiel and Isaiah doing their own thing. We do not see a connection. They seem to stand alone.

This is a major difference in the New Testament. In Ephesians 4, the Lord lists them alongside the other fivefold ministries. In the New Testament, the prophet is no longer a loner. You, prophets, may feel that you are alone all the time, but you are not called to be alone.

You are one of five, and you are meant to work with a team. That is the exciting part. Do you see why viewing the Old and New Testament prophet incorrectly has been putting pressure on you?

If you think that you need to be an Old Testament prophet, you think, "I am destined to be alone for the rest of my life. No one is ever going to understand me,

I am always going to have to go out and give a word that nobody wants to hear, and then go back home.

Am I ever going to get to the place where people actually listen to what I have to say, and I do not have to go from church to church or be kicked out and rejected?"

If you are thinking that you have to be like an Old Testament prophet, then there is no hope. However, in the New Testament, things have changed dramatically. We just need to catch up with the program.

God has been trying to get this message to us for a good couple hundred years already. Can we just get on board and get this Church built?

New Functions in the New Testament

There are a couple of new functions in the New Testament as well that we do not see at all in the Old Testament.

> *Acts 15:32 Now Judas and Silas, themselves being prophets also, exhorted and strengthened the brethren with many words.*

Never was this said of a prophet in the Old Testament. In the Old Testament, they mostly told people that they were going to die or that their bodies were going to rot.

"You are going to have plagues, stink, and lose your family." That is what the prophets usually prophesied in the Old Testament. There were not a whole lot of "feel good" prophecies going on back in the day.

Why not? It is because the Holy Spirit had not yet come. They did not know the grace of God. They did not know the price that Jesus would pay to cover them by His blood.

They only knew the righteousness of the Father. There was not a lot of exhorting going on in the Old Testament when the prophet spoke. People were afraid of the prophets.

They were terrified because what they spoke came to pass. They did not go to Samuel and say, "Let's sit down. It feels so good to be around you, Samuel. It is so nice. Let me hear some words of exhortation."

"Come on, Ezekiel, Amos, Micah, exhort me a little while."

I think that they lived a lonely life. Thank the Lord for His grace, His blood, and for the Holy Spirit. Prophets, we do not have to be alone forever. Praise you, Lord!

We are not meant to be alone. We are meant to be those who exhort and strengthen the Church. We are not meant to tear them down or convict them. That is the role of the Holy Spirit and the evangelist.

You have been trying to play evangelist, thinking, "I must separate the sheep from the goats. I must bring a sword and fire."

Broken Fixes Broken

However, there is a very tender heart beating inside of you. If there is one thing that every prophet has, it is that they have a passion for the brokenhearted and for those that have been abused and hurt.

You have such a desire to reach out and heal them, but you put on this stupid mask.

"I am a big, tough guy prophet. I am going to come in and say it as it is."

Would you let that go? Let the evangelist do that. God has put in you the heart of David. He has given you a heart after His own. He has given you tenderness and love, but you would not think so looking at a lot of the prophets today.

Why are you so tenderhearted? It is because you have a special relationship with Jesus. That is something that people should be jealous of. That is what they should see in you. It is His heart that He has put in your breast.

However, you have put so much junk on yourself - prophecies, visions, and revelations. You have piled yourself with so much, "I should do this, this, and this" that you have covered over the wounded heart that God wants to use.

You try to cover up your wounds, hurts, and vulnerability with a "Thus saith the Lord." Yet, you do not realize that it is your brokenness that is your testimony.

It is your brokenness that He has called. It is your brokenness that is going to heal a broken church. A church that needs to be strengthened, encouraged, and lifted up.

Let the evangelists bring that fire. You are not the fire bringer. You are the healer. You are meant to be bringing Jesus. That is why the Old and New Testament prophet are nothing alike.

> **The Old Testament prophets did not know Jesus. They did not introduce Jesus to Israel. They brought the Father's word to Israel, a very righteous word of God.**

There was no left or right. Yet, we have confused this.

You have so much passion in you. Because of the brokenness and love that you have, it is like a fire inside. If you view your calling through the Old Testament, you are going to come down so hard on the broken.

How many people have you broken by giving them the fire, instead of the oil and balm of healing that they needed?

We are so hyped up on the candy and on the big show that we forget that this is not how we are going to change the Church.

> ***Ephesians 4:12*** *For the equipping of the saints*
> *for the work of the ministry, for the edifying of*
> *the body of Christ,*
> *13 till we all come to the unity of the faith and of*
> *the knowledge of the Son of God, to a perfect*
> *man, to the measure of the stature of the fullness*
> *of Christ;*
> *14 that we should no longer be children, tossed*
> *to and fro and carried about with every wind of*
> *doctrine, by the trickery of men, in the cunning*
> *craftiness of deceitful plotting,*

See that one of the main tasks you have been given is to bring the knowledge of the Son of God. It is not the knowledge of the prophet or the knowledge of your doctrine. It is not the knowledge of your hobbyhorse or of your greatest revelation either.

Here is your calling, prophets, to equip, to build up, and to give people a living knowledge of Jesus.

Now, if you happen to use a prophetic word to do that, then that is fine and well. The teacher is going to use the Scriptures to do that, the evangelist is going to use the fire to do it, and you are going to use the love of Jesus to do that.

The Stripping has a Purpose

You are going to use the nature of Christ that has been born in you through the fire. That is why the prophet is stripped. Have you ever wondered why you were so stripped?

Of all the ministries, the prophet is stripped the most, and it is so that Christ can be seen in you.

Somewhere, in amongst all of your flesh, dross, and big mouth, underneath all the noise… is Jesus. God wants to get rid of the noise so that Jesus can come out.

Looking at the nature of Jesus when He walked the earth, we see that even John the Baptist did not get it.

Although John the Baptist knew that He was the Son of God, he was a little confused. Before he was killed, he sent some of his disciples to Jesus.

He told them to ask Jesus if He really was truly the one that was promised.

I can imagine that John was confused because he was the fire bringer, and Jesus did not fit into the kind of picture he had. He said of Jesus during his ministry, "The fire I have is nothing compared to the fire that is yet to come." He thought that the sinners were going to burn.

Imagine his confusion when he began watching Jesus perform miracles and sit with sinners! He must have thought, "Ok… He is eating with prostitutes. That was unexpected."

However, when Jesus went into the house of the tax collector, I think that is when it became a bit too much for John.

He must have thought, "Really? The IRS, Jesus? You love the IRS? The prostitute, I can understand, but the IRS? Are you sure you are the Son of God, because I was waiting for this fire?"

Jesus said to John's disciples, "Go and tell John what you see."

What did they see?

Jesus said, "The blind receive sight. The brokenhearted are healed. The lame walk."

Jesus brought healing. It is because you are so broken that God has called you to bring healing. He called you because of how unqualified you are.

You look at yourself and think, "Great! I am going to minister to this person that has the same problems as me. This is awesome, Lord."

You are so afraid to show that, so you put on the big, prophet thing. Don't you understand that this is what they need, and this is what the Lord is going to flow through?

You are meant to be equipping the saints, arming them, and adding things to them, but sometimes you are like John the Baptist that was hoping for a lot more fire to come down!

When you Get Your Lines Crossed

You go through the fire and death in your own life, and God requires so much of you sometimes that you make the mistake of thinking that God requires the same thing of everyone else.

God tells you to "die to your flesh", so you stand up and say to a new convert, "Die!"

The poor, new convert thinks, "Die? Why must I die? I just got born again, and I was actually kind of happy five minutes ago."

You think, "That is what God told me. So, clearly, this is a message for everyone."

One day I said, "Lord, is it too much for me to expect from everybody else what you expect from me?"

He said, "Yes, it is too much. To each one a grace has been given. That is not their piece of grace. Take your grace for yourself and go away with it and leave them to their piece of grace."

When you do this, somewhere in between, perhaps you will actually get some revelation as to what they are meant to be dealing with. When you share such a word, the people will be ready.

However, stop expecting everyone else to pass through the fire that you have passed through. You have passed through the fire so that they do not have to. Don't you get it?

Look at the teacher. Why did he have to face so many problems? Look at the evangelist. Why does he have to live such a holy life? Why is he separated so much?

This is so that God's people do not have to go through these things. You can give them the bottom line. Then, they can eat the fruit of your labor, and that fruit will remain.

Yet, we make the mistake of confusing our calling with our training and with the spiritual gifts. I really pray that I am bringing balance to all of that for you.

Office Vs. Calling

I do not just want to give you an office but help to bring out your calling. Yes, every prophet will share certain signs, and every evangelist will share certain signs, but each one of us has a different calling.

We will operate in that office in the way that God intends, with a mandate that is specific to each one of us, according to where God wants to put us in the grand scheme of things.

Do you not understand that the training and fire that you have gone through has shaped you, not just for this office, but for a lot more than that? This training has shaped you for your call so that God can put you in a specific environment that you might flourish in that environment.

He might take another prophet and raise him up separately and that prophet would not flourish in your environment, and you would not flourish in theirs. Side by side though, you will both be prophets, and you will share all of the signs of a prophet in office.

However, you are going to operate in accordance to how God has raised you. How can you put that pressure on everyone? It is the dispensation of grace that God has given you.

Find out what God requires of you and once you have that sorted, you can find out what God requires of others. Then, people will stop running away from you and stop being so outright terrified to see you crossing the room in their direction!

What Did I Say?!

I could not understand it. People would come by and visit and I would minister. They would spend hours talking to my husband, and I would say, "Hi," and they would look terrified and run away from me.

I thought, "What is wrong with me? Do I smell bad or something? Was it something I said?"

They were just terrified. They saw me preaching and from the pulpit, they were just terrified that I would come in and zero in on all of their sin. They thought that I would come and tell them to die to their flesh.

So, what I did was, took my dispensation of grace and gushed it out on you through this book instead, because the Lord told me that you could handle it!

The Lord told me that there was nothing wrong with my passion, but that I needed to put it in the right place. Putting this on a new convert is just a little too much.

I am so fiery and passionate. I remember a time when we were sharing the gospel with someone, and I just got fed up with what was going on and boldly stated, "This is just how it is…"

After I said that, Craig said, "Babe, this is an unbeliever. You could have maybe just tried to reach him with the love of Christ before trying to crucify his flesh."

However, that is the way that we, prophets, are wired, and so we think that everyone else is wired the same way. It is not so. This is why you need to go through the refining process.

This is the danger of putting somebody who can prophesy in office. They have not gone through that refining fire, and all it takes is the enemy to step in with a deception or a right or wrong kind of pressure that is not of God that will send them astray and unfortunately everyone else along with them.

We have to go through the preparation, training, and placement. If God does not place you in office, it simply means that you have not finished going through that refining. Your character is not ready yet.

BRINGING PERSPECTIVE TO THE MADDENING SPRINT TO OFFICE

Chapter 04 – Bringing Perspective to the Maddening Sprint to Office

As a prophet going through the training to reach office, it is not about how good or bad you are, or even how righteous or anointed you are. The question is, "Is your character at the place God needs it to be for the vision that He has given you?"

I want you to think about that.

We can get stuck on the fire God takes us through as prophets to the point where we forget that the fire has a very specific purpose. You see, it is not just about whether your character has been shaped or not. This stands to reason. If you have been experiencing fire... you are in a shaping process.

However, what you need to ask yourself is, "Has your character been shaped in accordance to the realm in which God wants to use you?"

Some people may go through it longer than others. Some may go through it shorter. It depends on where God wants to use that prophet. If He is using him in an environment that is going to temper his character in an extreme way, it is going to be a longer process.

What Kind of Sword are You Called to Be?

A good example is looking at how swords are made. You can make swords in various different ways. The Japanese knew how to make swords, and they are famous for them. Why is this?

They painstakingly hammer that steel and fold it and hammer it and fold it and hammer it. Then, they heat it and fold it and hammer it some more.

Now, there are different grades of swords. There are some that were made simply with a thin sheet of metal. That is practically a child's sword. Then, you have some that are folded once or twice.

However, there were those that are still famous today and being sold for millions of dollars. They were painstakingly created over time and in much fire, and they are very strong and very sharp... powerful swords in the hand of their master.

Which kind of sword do you want to be?

> **We complain about the process and fire that we go through, but every sword has a place and a function for a specific kind of warfare. Sometimes, we need to go through the refining process a little bit longer to shape us into what we need to become to do that particular call that God has called us to do.**

Everybody is trying to rush to prophetic office. They say, "I'll take a sword, any sword. Just make me a sword!"

So you add to the shaping God is trying to do in your life, and you come out as a broad sword. The problem is that the Lord wants to use you in a completely different environment where maybe a dagger is needed - something sharp and pointy.

Now, here you are, a big, fat, broad sword that is of no use to anyone. You are a broad sword in the wrong place. Allow God to do the shaping in your character according to what He wants you to do.

I have seen so many prophets go through training. While the phases are the same, (Brook Cherith, Zarephath, and Carmel) the character that it brings out of each prophet is different.

(These phases are covered in more detail in the *Prophetic Boot Camp* book)

Each prophet faces a different kind of death. For some, God deals with your spirit of rebellion. For another, God deals with your dependence on your family. For others, God deals with the fact that you judge everyone or that you have a deep root of bitterness.

Whatever it is, each one of us has something that needs shaping. The phases are the same, but what God makes you into is quite different from your fellow prophet. That is what is so beautiful. You are not "just a prophet".

You are unique in His sight. Allow Him to make you unique. That is what will equip the saints. That is what is going to give you the tools to build them up. So, please stop despising the fire.

Do Not Despise the Fire

"There is so much more training still before I can finally get to office."

You say that as if when you get to office that it will get easier. No, the training you go through in preparation prepares you for the rigors of standing in prophetic office. This is not a race guys! This is not a marathon where you achieve the prize, get to grab a snack and a juice box, and then take it easy while you watch the other runners make it to the finish line.

Don't you get it? Everything you are facing in your training phase is boot camp! It is preparing you for the real battle. Everything you are going through right now is in a safe environment of training. To prepare you, shape you, and equip you for what lies ahead.

Today is Preparing you For Tomorrow

When you qualify and the Holy Spirit gives you that authority, that is when the real battlefield is set before you, and you get a taste of the true pressure that you will face as a prophet. I want to clear this up even before I move on to the signs of the prophet in office, because as I start showing you what you will be, you will understand what is going on in your life right now.

What spiritual warfare are you facing right now? What pressures are you facing right now? Don't you realize that if you face these pressures correctly right now, in the fire, that when you step into the fullness of your office you will make those wise decisions by instinct?

You see, right now you have to think everything through. You are like a new recruit in the army. You are still learning to use your weapons. Your trigger finger is not trained. Your muscle memory is non-existent. You do not have the instinct for war just yet.

That is why these choices seem so hard right now. It is organic for you to follow after your flesh. It feels more natural to rebel than to submit. It is easier for you to run away from the pressure than towards it.

Your very spiritual instinct is for self-preservation instead of displaying self-control and selflessness. That is why you are facing what you are. The good news is that this is a muscle memory that can be learned!

Right now, in this exact pressure situation, you can allow the Holy Spirit to condition you to make the right choices. Soon those biblical and "fruit of the spirit" choices will become second nature to you. When you experience rejection, you will respond in self-control. When someone hits you on the one cheek, you will offer the other.

These "difficult" responses to you right now, if you allow God to work, will become your "easy peasy" later on when you stand in office.

Spiritual Muscle Memory

How many more untrained commanders do we need on the field? Commanders that react with a firestorm of bitterness when opposed and with a dart of anger when rejected?

We all enjoy a little bit of self-indulgence, don't we? We think to ourselves, "Yes, I know I need to deal with my pride. Yes, I know that I must combat this bad temper of mine, however, when it counts, I know I will make the right decision."

No, you won't!

In fact, that pressure situation will come at you so hard and fast, all the bad reactions will come out of you at the same time! So yes, right now, it's time to embrace the pressure. Not just because you want to reach office. Not just because you want more spiritual revelation. Not because you need to wear the title. You do it, because you want that spiritual muscle memory.

When the Lord tells you to take aim at the enemy, you must be so proficient in the spirit that you take out the target and not an ally. Do not count on yourself to "get it right next time." You won't.

Do not think that, "It will be easier next time when I am more at peace." No, it won't!

The flesh is the flesh, and the Holy Spirit knows exactly what is in you. And by the way... so does the enemy!

So, when is the best time to practice the correct responses in a pressure situation? The answer is a tad obvious. When they come up! The last thing you want to do right now is run around and start digging out all your dirt (Yup... I called it! We prophets are all alike!)

The moment you say, "Something needs to change." The prophet in us gets a shovel and starts digging. There is most definitely an easier way. The Lord has already been pointing His finger on what He needs you to work on. In fact, it's simple.

What pressure situation are you facing right now? Is it rejection from a spouse? Is it more work than you can handle? Are people making unfair demands on you and giving you no reward for all that hard work?

Everyone else gets it easy, but you do not?

Your boss takes an instant disliking to you for no reason.

Your pastor acts out of the norm and just starts coming down hard on you.

Your finances suddenly take a dive.

Your sibling starts getting on your case and picking a fight with you.

Your wife starts acting irrational and making demands you cannot meet.

Your children turn their backs on you after all you invested into them.

No one is there for you. No one understands. You feel alone...

Yes, prophet – you are not alone. You are not the first prophet in training to face these pressures, and you will not be the last! The point of this discussion though is not about what pressures you are facing, but rather how you are responding to them!

What does your muscle memory look like right now? How have you trained your mind, emotions and will? When rejection hits, what is your instantaneous response? When you are overworked, what is your immediate reaction?

Is this a godly reaction? Are you reacting like God needs you to right now? Are you the right kind of sword?

> *2 Timothy 2:19 Nevertheless the solid foundation of God stands, having this seal: "The Lord knows those who are His," and, "Let everyone who names the name of Christ depart from iniquity."*
> *20 But in a great house there are not only*

vessels of gold and silver, but also of wood and clay, some for honor and some for dishonor.
21 Therefore if anyone cleanses himself from the latter, he will be a vessel for honor, sanctified and useful for the Master, prepared for every good work.

So what kind of sword do you want to be? The Lord knows those who are His and if you are one that names Christ as your Savior, then it is for you to depart from iniquity. Do you know what iniquity is? It's not just sin.

Here is a section from the Strong's Concordance definition for you:

> adikia; from 94;
>
> (legal) injustice (properly, the quality, by implication, the act);
>
> morally, wrongfulness (of character, life or act)

Iniquity is more than just one little sin. It is the nature of sin. It is the character that you are. It's more than a bad habit. It's more than the cuss word you let out. It's more than the spat of anger you let get the better of you.

This is a sinful character that controls you. A spiritual muscle memory, if you will, that reacts naturally in a given set of circumstances.

2 Timothy 2:19 tells us to flee from iniquity! In other words – flee from the sinful character within you! It

means running away from the old man and towards the new. Away from your bad reactions and right into the fire so that the Holy Spirit can burn off that dross and give you righteousness in its place.

This happens so that when you stand in office, and the Lord needs you most, Jesus comes out and not your iniquity. I have not even got on to the good part yet though. Keep reading, and you will see that the Word tells us that when we flee from iniquity, we become vessels of honor!

God chooses us to be vessels of gold and silver in His house. So I ask you again, what kind of sword do you want to be?

Do you want to be a vessel of honor or dishonor? Well now, that depends entirely on how much "fleeing" you do from your nature of iniquity! The more we put aside the old man and allow the Holy Spirit to sanctify us and shape us, we are told that we will be made into vessels of honor – used for every good work!

You – The Shape Shifter

Now, remember I shared how you are a broad sword but the Lord might need a dagger for a specific situation? Well, once you get used to that shaping process and reach prophetic office, you will discover something quite amazing.

You will discover that not only has the Lord been spending a lot of time making you into a very specific kind of vessel, but He has also been teaching you to shape shift!

By going through this shaping process, you have learned to flee from iniquity. You have learned to let go of "self". You have learned to hear the voice of your Savior, and you have begun to move with Him.

How much easier then, will it be, to change shape again later on? When you reach prophetic office, you will have gained the muscle memory for a specific task through intense training. This means that you know how to train. You know how to go through the process. Fantastic! Office qualifies you to go through it again... but without all that kicking and screaming this time.

Do not think that once you reach prophetic office that you stay the same kind of vessel – not unless you want to be stuck in one place your entire life, always ministering to the same kinds of people! Different people need a different kind of minister. Different jobs require a different vessel, and you can expect the Lord to shape you again and again.

So please, do not rush your training process. Train hard and train in wisdom. Learn each lesson. Do not be so quick to rush through it that you forget the main point of it all – to prepare you for the real battlefield!

The qualification is to face a warfare you have never faced before. So, take your time to make sure that you are sharp enough! Do you recognize the hand of God on your life? Do you recognize when He is putting you through your paces and calling you to react in righteousness instead of in iniquity?

Have you taken enough time to develop your spiritual muscle memory? Do you respond with faith, hope, and love, when you are in your place of weakness? If not, take your time to develop this weakness now, because you will certainly not have the time to do it later.

Take a moment, before moving on to the next chapter, to look at the pressure situations you are in right now. They might be financial, spiritual, relational, or simply emotional. The pressure situation itself is not really the problem.

Now, what is your "knee jerk" reaction to each of these situations? What comes out of you before you can slap your hand over your mouth and shut yourself up? This is what the Lord is working on right now. He is exposing your iniquity, not to shame you, but so that you have a clear picture of what you need to flee from!

Face Your Reality

Facing our reality as prophets is one of the greatest gifts we can give ourselves. We try so hard to prove to ourselves, the Lord and everyone else, what our worth is, that we are too afraid to look at our nature of iniquity.

So we go around in circles while the Lord tries to point it out. Let's make this simple and please... let's get away from circling that mountain in the desert. It's just too tiresome!

Face the fact that you do not handle your pressure well. Face the reality of what comes out of you when you are faced with that pressure situation. Pick that iniquity up in your hands and take a good, hard look at it.

Own it. Recognize it. Then, put it down and flee from it! You cannot flee from something you never acknowledge! You cannot scrape dross off gold, if you refuse to even admit that there is any dross present! Facing your reality will speed this training process up and help you develop that spiritual muscle memory quickly!

1. Identify your pressure situation
2. Identify your automatic response to that pressure situation
3. Face your reality
4. Flee iniquity
5. Replace that iniquity with a righteous muscle memory that will come out of you automatically when it counts!

THE PROPHETIC OFFICE PROFILE

Chapter 05 – The Prophetic Office Profile

There is quite a difference between someone called to be a prophet and someone who is standing in the fullness of prophetic office.

When the Lord Jesus finds us in the wombs of our mothers, we do not have a lot to give to Him. However, through time, He shapes us. He leads us into situations and gears us towards the call that we finally discover on our lives.

The truth is though that the Lord Jesus is not the only one at work. The enemy has certainly had a part to play in many of the hurtful things you have faced in your life and as a result, he has left some scars.

This tug of war, if you will, leaves you with some character traits that need some work before you reach office. So what we look like when we recognize the call of God on our lives and who we are once we are ready to walk that call out are two very different people.

I am making this point because I have covered in extensive detail what someone called to be a prophet looks like. All of us have a certain orientation. Many of us share similar hurts and ambitions.

I called these "Signs of the Prophetic Call" in some of my other books namely, *Practical Prophetic Ministry* and *Prophetic Essentials*.

However, in this book, I will not be sharing on the signs of the prophetic call. Instead, I will be sharing on the signs of today's prophet in office!

In other words, we are going to fast forward and take a bit of a look at what the prophetic warrior looks like once he has been through boot camp! What is the character of a prophet in office and how will you know if you are standing in the fullness of that office?

Well, that is what I am dedicating the rest of this book to.

Now, before I start rattling off these signs, one at a time, I want you to take a moment to consider some of the pressure situations you have been facing. Particularly those that you started looking at in the previous chapter.

Recognize the character that the Lord is trying to shape in you according to the signs I share here. Sure, I cannot take away the fire, but I can certainly give you hope and something to look forward to.

I do not know about you, but I am the kind of person that just needs to know that God has got this and that this training has a purpose. I do not care how tough it is or how much fire I go through – if I know that all of that fire is in the hand of God and has a purpose – I am ready for anything.

I get the feeling that you are the same. So let's do it!

The First Signs That you are Ready

So then, what does it look like when you have "arrived"?

The answer to this is easy. You do not think that you have arrived. That is usually the first sign that you are getting ready to enter office. When you have finally "arrived", you do not feel that you have arrived, and you do not feel that you deserve to "arrive".

You are actually embarrassed to say that you are a prophet. You say, "God has called me to be a…" and then you whisper the word "…prophet".

The new recruit went around shouting, "I am called to be a prophet to the nations! Watch out people, here come my revelations."

When I hear that, I say, "You enjoy that while you can. Boot camp is coming…"

It is because when you really stand in prophetic office, you are too scared to say that too loudly, in case the lightning strikes, and your flesh gets sizzled for being a little too prideful.

I should have made that sign 1 because it is so true. You just say, "I am a minister of God."

The fire that you go through and the price that you pay brings you to such a conclusion of His grace that when you stand up, your knees are knocking.

I look back at when I first started flowing in the prophetic and I was so bold. I was as bold as a lion. I prophesied to everyone. I was ready to get out there and change the world.

I was excited about the gifts and everything God was showing me. Then, you go through the fire, and you are hammered and folded and hammered and folded... repeatedly!

After that, I stood up in fear and trembling. My knees were knocking, my hands were shaking, and I said, "Lord, I feel like a child. What is wrong with me? By now, I should be seasoned."

However, I felt so unsalted because I realized that if the Holy Spirit did not move, I had nothing to say. I would stand in front of these people and look like an idiot. My calling and ability to operate in the anointing did not depend on me – it depended on Jesus.

If He did not want to use this vessel, He did not need to! The gifts are not mine, the grace is not mine, the anointing is not mine. All I have is Jesus, and there is nothing left. I stand naked. All I have is Jesus.

Jesus is Reflected

If Jesus does not pitch up, I have nothing. So, you know you are starting to get ready when you are not so bold anymore to say, "Hey, check me out, guys."

It is because that fire has brought about the reality of Christ in you. It has brought about the reality of His grace. You stand up and say,

"Lord, you are still going to use me? You saw what I did. You saw who I was. You saw how broken I was, and you would still dare to use me?"

That is what a prophet in office looks like.

The Prophetic Office Profile

Sign #1 Powerful Function in Prayer and Decree

A prophet in office functions strongly in prayer and decree - and not in front of the church. He does not need you to hear his word to know that it is going to come to pass.

He does not even need to prophesy anymore, and that is why I did not say "prophecy". I said, "Prayer and Decree".

When I give forth a decree in this earth, I do not tell you. I watch it happen. I do not need to tell you. It is not my word. It is God's word. When He sends forth a word, it does not return void.

It does just like it did for Samuel, the word goes forth and it happens. The prophet in office says, "Good. I have done my job. Do I need you to praise me for it? Please don't! It is embarrassing. It is not my word. I cannot take credit for a word that was not my origination, but rather it was the Lord's."

I would not take one of my favorite books of the Bible, sign my name on it, and say, "Check it out. Isn't that cool?" now would I?

Credit Goes to God Alone

So then, how can I take credit for any prophetic word that God gives me? All I can boast in is that I was weak and foolish enough and that I knew how to die. That is all. He gives the word.

The prophet operates very strongly in decree. He tears down and builds up. When he sends forth that word as a decree, whether you hear it or not, it takes place because he sent forth a power into this earth.

That is the authority that the prophet gets when they get to office. That is why you need the refining process I spoke about in the previous chapter. Take someone that has been born again for a couple of months. Are you going to give them this kind of authority? Are you kidding me?

Do you think that I am going to give my five-year-old son a loaded gun? Do you think I am going to say, "Go ahead and get the squirrels, sweetheart?"

He has a little toy gun, and he pretends to shoot the squirrels that are eating mommy's grass. However, I do not say, "I see that you know how to use a gun. Let me give you the real thing. Go and get that squirrel, baby."

Why are we doing that with the prophets in the Church? We are giving them loaded guns, and they are decreeing tsunamis, death, and destruction. Then, they say, "Look, it happened."

No duh! You spoke it forth. What do you think you are doing with your mouth? Giving a prophetic word is not an F.Y.I. You are releasing a power when you speak. You have the indwelling of the Holy Spirit.

Now, you add some anointing to that, even if it is a contaminated anointing, and you are releasing power from your mouth. Don't you get that? (I cover this in more detail in the *Prophetic Warrior* and *Prophetic Counter Insurgence*, so I will not labor the point of "contamination" here.)

So, you better have been refined by the fire before you get up and start tearing down. You cannot go wrong with building up, but if you are saying, "In the name of Jesus, I close that ministry down", you better have gone through the fire so you know you are speaking for God and not the enemy.

You better know when you decree that it is God speaking and not you. You better know that you are not decreeing this word because of your own preconceived ideas.

Paul said, "I handed them over to satan for the destruction of the flesh." (1 Corinthians 5:5)

You better know what you are doing when you speak such a decree. I do not like speaking such decrees out front where everyone can see them, because I am doing so in fear and trembling.

I know that when I speak, things are going to happen. A prophet in office has that kind of authority. Their words are not just "have a nice day" kind of words. They are words that create.

There are so many prophets that can say, "God says you are going to be blessed, God says you are going to get married, God says this new job is going to work out."

That is simple prophetic ministry. My teenager can minister like that. What sets the prophet apart? He does not say, "God says that whatever your hand touches is going to be blessed."

He says, "In the name of Jesus, that work will be blessed. I call forth those circumstances and materials. I birth that work in the spirit right now, and I call it to begin to flourish and rise up.

I cut away the things that were, and I raise up right now, in the name of Jesus, the things that will be. I call it in accordance to the pattern that the Lord has set and that which is in the heavens will be manifest on earth right now, in Jesus name."

That is decree. I do not care whether you like it or not or hear it or not. So, prophet, do not tell me that "this" is what you think God is doing. Speak it forth. That is what a prophet is meant to do. He is not meant to tickle your ears.

Why Prophetic Words Do Not Come to Pass

Why do some prophetic words never come to pass? It is because they are never spoken forth but simply given as an F.Y.I.

"For your interest, this is what God thinks."

I could have heard that in my journal during my private time with the Lord. What do I need you for?

Prophets, we embarrass ourselves. I have been there, so I understand. Often during a seminar, a well-meaning prophet in training will come and share with me, "God gives me this prophetic word for you."

I appreciate the heart because I see that underneath all of that need for recognition, acceptance, and love, there is a heart that loves the Lord. So, I am happy to say, "Thank you, my sister."

Truth is though, I have a team that is ready to seek the Lord on my behalf should I ever need it. I know that not all ministries are the same, but in ours, we kinda bump into prophets on the way to the kitchen. (Most literally!)

However, what I often need more than a prophetic word is a spoken word of decree. See, I can never have enough of those! Creative words of power that cause things that are not to come to pass. To bring heaven to earth!

Can we please have some prophets that stop tickling the ears and start sending forth a creative force into this earth that will build and establish the End-Times Church?

We are so busy trying to entertain the End-Times Church that we have forgotten that the foundation is on the prophets and apostles, and we are meant to be building the End-Times Church and leaving a foundation that remains.

Mixing It all Up

I think many under-estimate the power of decree. I think about how often people come to share not only their prophetic words, but also their business advice, team counsel, and direction in "the name of the Lord". Many think that if they baptize it with "spirituality" that it gives their opinion more of a punch.

And so you use your prophetic revelation to try and twist the arm of the person you are trying to reach. You feel that if you are anointed enough, you will eventually change their minds from doing things their way.

If you give them just the right prophetic word, they will change their minds and run their ministry differently. If you share the right dream with them, then you will convince them to ordain those you feel need to be ordained or that they will re-organize the ministry finances how you feel they should organize them.

I think you are missing the point. The power of decree bypasses all that. Why are you trying so hard to change the minds of the people when it is within your power to change their circumstances and their hearts?

Leave it to the teachers to re-educate and to lay the doctrinal foundation, and you do your job correctly. The Lord is already fleshing this out in you right now. The pressures and even a lot of the rejections that you are facing are gearing you to become conformed to the prophetic office archetype!

The kind of archetype that when you decree – things happen. Why beat around the bush trying to convince the pastor or ministry leader that they must do what God wants, when you could go to the Throne Room and decree, under His authority, the plans that need to be set in motion?

I have personally witnessed the power of this kind of authority. I have met prophets in office that are sent to a church for such an assignment. Many times, they are not even known by the leadership. However, they will stand at the back of the hall after every single meeting and simply decree God's will into the church.

One such lady spent a number of years in a church releasing decrees for the Spirit of God to move. For the gifts of the Spirit to manifest and for an apostolic covering to be brought to the church. Massive shifts started to take place. The Holy Spirit started showing up in the meetings and before long, the pastor of the church stepped down and handed over to an apostle, who began to re-structure the church into a fivefold ministry pattern. Something that this prophet had foreseen and had been decreeing for years.

Once her assignment was over, the Lord shifted her to another church with another set of instructions. Only a prophet in office can bring about this kind of shift.

Bring on the Power

Prophets, when you are dead and gone, what will you have left behind? Will it be a tombstone that says, "She was born, she prophesied, she died"?

Or, to be more accurate... She resurrected and died and resurrected and died until she finally just died.

Please, Lord, can something more be said of me one day? What are we building that remains? A prophet in office is meant to be building the Church. We are meant to be equipping and leaving something behind. The words of decree that we speak have the creative power to build something that remains long until after we are gone!

Prophetic Orientation vs. Prophetic Office

It is one thing to have a prayer orientation and another to send out decrees that change the course of a church or ministry! This is probably the greatest shift you will recognize as you enter into prophetic office.

When you first come to a realization of your call, you are drawn into prayer. You feel an intimacy with Jesus, and many who have a prophetic orientation have a fire for the ministry of intercession. There are many who do not progress past this point and are used powerfully by the Lord as an intercessor in their local church.

Some stay at home and continue to pray as God leads them, and I have seen incredible fruit of such prayer warriors. However, this is simply an orientation to the prophetic. Someone who functions in prophetic ministry. Being an intercessor does not automatically place you into prophetic office.

You might begin there, but as the Holy Spirit takes you through the fire, you become sharper, and once placed in office, you receive a level of authority that increases the power of your prayer.

Sign #2 Spiritual Warfare at the Highest Level

A prophet in office will also engage in spiritual warfare at the highest level. You will do warfare on behalf of the Church. Again, this is not something that is done up front where everyone can see you.

You are going to do warfare on behalf of God's people because you wrestle not with flesh and blood, but with principalities in high places (Ephesians 6:12). That is the role of the prophet.

You are on the front lines. It is like in the days of Nehemiah where you have a trowel in one hand and a sword in the other. You will do warfare with one hand and build up with the other. That is what the prophet looks like.

He is doing warfare, but not out there saying, "Come and check me out doing warfare." You are not an Old Testament prophet. You are not Elijah. You do not need anybody to see your glory.

By the way, Elijah was tearing down the prophets of Baal. He was not trying to impress. Who are you trying to impress?

Our warfare is done at the highest level. If you are tearing down, building, birthing, and decreeing, you are going to start coming against some demonic attack.

Satan has a pattern and plan of his own that he is trying to implement. Before God can have His way in this earth, we need somebody that will push against those plans of the enemy and give God license.

That is why a lot of your job is done through spiritual warfare. It is for this reason that we implemented something we call "The Prayer Wall" in our ministry. No, it does not have anything to do with Jerusalem. Someone asked me that once. I thought I would clarify it so that when I mention it again, you know what I am talking about.

We borrowed a page out of the book of Nehemiah. Just as Nehemiah built a wall to protect the city and the temple within it, the prophets are also called to build a spiritual wall and to protect the work of God.

We are to be watchmen on that wall, but before we can be watchmen, the wall needs to be built. So, there is a season of building and establishing and then a season of standing on that wall every single moment of the day to watch out for the enemy and to do warfare to protect the people of God.

This is a wall where the prophets are working in one hand and decreeing in the other. It's a beautiful picture of how the prophet does warfare with one hand and establishes God's plan with the other. That is the role of the prophet.

Prophetic Orientation vs. Prophetic Office

One of the greatest shifts in spiritual warfare when you reach office is that the kind of warfare you engage in does not remain restricted to your inner circle any longer. It goes beyond the boundaries of your family, ministry, or church. Rather the Lord will use you to wrestle on His behalf. You will be as Daniel who sought God for an entire nation!

Like Abraham who interceded for an entire city. Like Moses who prayed for an entire nation to be saved. (I cover this in more detail in the *Calling the Prophets to Arms* message. Look out for it on YouTube or www.ami-bookshop.com)

Sign #3 Identifies Believer's Ministries

One of the main functions of the prophet is to help people find where they belong.

The pastor creates an environment, right? He gives them a place where they feel like they belong. Then, the prophet comes along and says, "I see the body ministry of leadership in this member."

Prophet and Pastor Working Hand in Hand

Then, the pastor says, "Perfect, I know exactly where to put them."

It is beautiful. The prophet and the pastor, in the correct pattern, are a fantastic team. You would not say so looking at the Church today, but the Lord is bringing such a resurrection in the Church right now.

I am seeing pastors with a true pastor's heart rise up. They are working with prophets in this way, and this is exactly how it should be.

The pastors need to create the environment, but the prophets need to help them identify where each member of that body belongs so that they can be slotted correctly in place.

Prophetic Orientation vs. Prophetic Office

It is one thing to have a passion for everyone to belong and another to have the authority and revelation to put them into place. When you first come to a conviction of your calling, it burns in you to see every believer in place.

You go to church, and you become frustrated with those who are rejected and cast aside. You are frustrated to see a Body that is limp and only a few of its members alive and participating. Having this desire is certainly a sign of your prophetic call. Back then, you had a prophetic orientation, and you had a long journey to go on.

However, having the position, authority, and wisdom to now put those individuals in place takes someone in prophetic office. This is the place where God is taking you, and this is why you go through the training you do. To put your own ideas aside so that when you are in place, you can efficiently help God's people identify where they belong.

It does not end there though. Once you have identified their place, it is for you to release them into it. This may require a word of decree to release the anointing and gifts of the Spirit into them. It might mean actually training them up in that position. It might mean working with the leadership directly to ensure that their place is secured.

You are going a lot further now than just having a "wish and a dream" of everyone having a place in the church. A prophet in office is positioned, anointed, and equipped to put those members into place correctly.

Sign #4 Active in Anointing, Appointing and Equipping

He is also active in anointing and appointing. If someone needs to be placed in prophetic office, the prophet should be doing it. Actually, the prophet and the pastor should be doing it together.

I taught on this in *Today's Pastor*. The prophet and the pastor should be laying on hands and appointing people to office, releasing gifts and ministries, decreeing gifts of revelation, and whatever else is needed for that believer to be equipped for the call on his life.

Why is this? It is because the saints need to be equipped. How else are they not going to be windswept by all those doctrines, unless you do a bit of decreeing over their lives?

Not only should you be helping to identify their place, but you should be releasing that ministry on them, through the power of decree.

I am reminded of David fleeing from Saul. He ran to Samuel who took him under his wing and protected him until he was able to claim the sword of Goliath and escape to the Cave of Adullam. Samuel did a lot more than simply anoint David - he also equipped him to do his job!

As a prophet in office, being an example and mentor will become part and parcel of your ministry functions. Not only will you be teaching people how to enter into a face-to-face relationship with Jesus, but the Lord will use you very practically in their callings.

It means a lot more than saying a prophetic word and leaving town. It means sticking around long enough after the anointing to continue equipping. So, you have identified where a person belongs. You have decreed, and you have put them into place. What now?

There is a lot more involved in fulfilling your call than just being given a task or a position. You of all people should know that. No, it is going to take a leader and a prophet in office to take such a person under the wings and to show them the ropes for a while.

To give them the skills that God has given to you. To help them flap their little baby wings until they can fly. As prophets, we can get a little too spiritual sometimes. We are so bent on giving everyone the insight into the Spirit that we sometimes forget that they have to function in this very real world.

Do not stop at helping someone identify where they belong, train them in the place that they have been appointed to!

Be like Barnabas, who took Mark under his wings and showed him the ropes.

Prophetic Orientation vs. Prophetic Office

This certainly separates someone who has a prophetic orientation and someone who is in prophetic office. Even someone with the gift of prophecy can get revelation on where a person belongs, but it takes an appointed prophet to equip them for the task.

This goes far beyond having wisdom or getting a word from God. It means taking hold of the word of God and implementing it practically. If you are unable to train the person in the place that God has given to them, then it is for you to help them find someone who can.

You are the one who is called to anoint, appoint, and to equip! So, work with the pastor. Work with your apostle, but do not quit until you see the entire process through.

If you know any prophets in office, or if you are in office yourself, you already feel this fire in you. You are not content to sit on the sidelines and watch things happen. You are not content to just get a revelation. You are waiting for the orders to run into the fray and to engage.

Your training equips you to do just that. You will learn to work with the fivefold ministry. You will learn submission. You will learn teamwork. And then, you will play a vital part in equipping the Church!

FURTHER IDENTIFYING THE PROPHET IN OFFICE

Chapter 06 – Further Identifying the Prophet in Office

I know that I have labored the reality of the prophetic fire, but before pressing in with more signs of the prophet in office, I want to clarify something.

The point of this all is to be a doer! Let me remind you of this fantastic scripture:

> **James 1:25** *But he who looks into the perfect law of liberty and continues in it, and is not a forgetful hearer but a doer of the work, this one will be blessed in what he does.*

When the call of God becomes real to you, you look around with a passion to change everything that is wrong. You want to be the one who does something about it. You become frustrated about the lack of inaction in the Church.

How surprising it was for you then, when the Lord not only confirmed your call, but also sent you directly to the wilderness! From having a passion to "do", you are told to sit down, be quiet, and listen! So much for "doing!"

This is probably the greatest transition between training and walking in prophetic office. When you finally come to the place of being content with sitting for hours in the presence of Jesus and taking time in your prayer closet, the way opens up and you begin to… do, do, do!

In fact, the transition can be a little shocking. Just as shocking as it was when the Lord stripped you and told you to sit down! For a long season, you learn how to flow in the gifts, develop your relationship with Jesus, and allow the Holy Spirit to change your character. It is because of this that you now qualify to start doing some real work.

I am not talking about interpreting a dream or giving the odd prophetic word. I am talking about bringing about real change in the Church. You transition from student to being a "doer of the work" as James so beautifully expresses it here.

So, are you ready yet? Well that depends on where you are in your training. But… we are not here to talk about that right now. We are here to look at what the prophet in office looks like. So, let's move on to the next sign, which is:

Sign #5 Ministry to the Universal Church

The ministry of the prophet in office is to the universal church. It is not just to the local church. To give you a brief explanation: The universal church encompasses the Church as a whole. The local church refers to your local church family, your "base" so to speak. While Peter's church base was Jerusalem, he was sent out to the universal church and reached the Church all over Europe.

The prophet is likely to have a church base, but he is going to move around.

He is helping people to find their place, and I am sure that there are only so many fivefold ministers in your local church for you to help identify. There are only so many gifts and ministries that you can point out and then your job is done.

So, let's go and do that in the rest of the Church world as well, shall we? And so that is why the prophet in office's ministry extends to the universal (international) Church.

Samuel is also a fantastic example of this. He ministered in a circuit. He was not always at home, but he did have a base that he returned to and hung up his coat, so to speak.

Now I know that prophets have a reputation for being loners, but those days are going to be fast behind you. Not only will the Lord plug you back into a local church, but He will also open the doors to extend your ministry reach.

Samuel might have been restricted to the temple as a child, but when his time came, the Lord released him. The same is for you. There are many prophets in training that are called to isolation for a season. You leave your church. You are cut off. Just when you get content with your lot in life, you qualify, and the Lord sends you back to the local church.

Depending on your mandate, the Lord may decide to keep you there to reach out from that base, but He will also open up other doors. There is a lot to be said about prophetic types, but I am not going to get sidetracked on that now. For now, cling to this encouragement – you are meant to be a part of a whole.

You are just one of the fivefold ministry, and the Lord intends for you to be plugged in and efficiently fulfilling the mandate He has placed on your life.

Prophetic Orientation vs. Prophetic Office

Now, someone who is in prophetic ministry will function in the local church. If you are in a local ministry right now, that is fine.

You are still in training and prophetic ministry, but know that when you get into office, a shift is going to take place. God is going to start moving you around.

I will mention here briefly that not everyone is called to office. There are some that God will keep in prophetic ministry. This is for those who are called to prophetic office. (For more on this refer to *Prophetic Boot Camp*, Chapters 8 and 11)

Sign #6 Relationship with Jesus

> *2 Corinthians 2:14 Now thanks be to God who always leads us in triumph in Christ, and through us diffuses the fragrance of His*

knowledge in every place.
15 For we are to God the fragrance of Christ
among those who are being saved and among
those who are perishing.

If you read *Today's Evangelist*, then you will know how
I spoke about what defines the evangelist is his
relationship with the Holy Spirit.

Well, what defines a true prophet is their relationship
with Jesus. If you see someone stand up and talk all
about how everyone needs to know Jesus and come
into His presence and come to their groom and the
lover of their soul, then you are listening to a prophet.

The evangelist brings the Holy Spirit's fire. You see
manifestations of healings, miracles, and many other
manifestations (demonic and Holy Spirit led!). While
there are many that have a grace message, there is no
doubt that they want to see the work of the Holy Spirit
in your life. They do not talk about relationship as
much as the fruit that should be manifest in your life.
This stands to reason, because the Holy Spirit is the
one that acts on the creation – He is the one that
moves His hands and causes a creation to take place.

However, the prophet stands up and just wants you to
grasp this one concept: Jesus. Jesus is here, and He is
everything. He is the lover of your soul. He is your
groom.

The prophet is spouting from Song of Solomon and
getting poetic on you. Why? It is because he has such

intimacy with Jesus. When you love someone so much and experience Him as you do when you go through this kind of training, you are going to talk about Him.

When you are broken to the core and see Jesus, and you know as you are known, Jesus is all over your face. How can you not talk about somebody that you are so passionately in love with?

When you see someone passionately in love with Jesus, and their eyes are sparkling like they just came out of the most romantic encounter with Him, you are looking at a prophet.

This is somebody that knows Jesus. That is the power of your call. Don't you get that? The Church does not know Jesus like you know Him. They need to know Him like that. They need the knowledge of the Son of God that you have received.

Prophetic Orientation vs. Prophetic Office

Your call began with a hunger for Jesus. You sought Him, and you found Him. As you were drawn into training, the veils were removed, and you began to know Him as you never did. Your hunger and thirst were met until you came to the place where you and Jesus could sit all alone in a room, and you were completely content.

It is this relationship that forges the foundation of your call, and a prophet in office does not just talk about revelations and grand visions. He talks from the perspective of a personal encounter. For example, I could give you a list of instructions my husband gave me. I could tell you the kind of things he likes to do. This might tell you the kind of man he is, to a point.

However, when I talk about my husband, I talk from a perspective of being one with him. I am flesh of his flesh, and I know what his desires are. I speak as an extension of him. This is the defining line of your relationship with Jesus, when you first start out and as you go through the process to enter into office.

I wish that I could say that every prophet does this right, but there are many who do not take the time to work through their hurts and frustrations enough to enter into this knowledge of Christ.

> ***Ephesians 3:17*** *that Christ may dwell in your hearts through faith; that you, being rooted and grounded in love,*
> *18 may be able to comprehend with all the saints what is the width and length and depth and height—*
> *19 to know the love of Christ which passes knowledge; that you may be filled with all the fullness of God.*

To truly be filled with the "fullness of God" means coming to understand the reality of His love. Not to know of it. Not to study it. Not even to explain it. It means to live it. For it to saturate every part of you that no matter what storms come, and what rejections you face, it anchors you. You become an extension of Jesus.

You see the lost and broken and reach out as His extension. Not because you get revelation. Not because it is the right thing to do. You do it out of the immeasurable agape love that is established in your spirit through the face-to-face relationship with Jesus.

There is only one way to walk in agape love, and it is not to "work it up". It means to have a daily encounter with Jesus. The prophet in office has this encounter, because without it, He has no power to "do" all the functions I have listed here so far.

Love is indeed the powerful force behind the ministry of the prophet. Without it, he is a clanging symbol and a cloud without rain.

Sign #7 Anointing for the Ministry of Inner Healing

> ***Romans 12:15*** *Rejoice with those who rejoice, and weep with those who weep.*

When you know Jesus like I just described, you feel His heart, and you are going to weep with those who weep and rejoice with those who rejoice. You are not going to do it because you are "in touch with your emotions", but you minister because you feel His heart.

You will find yourself ministering to someone that looks hard as a rock, and suddenly your heart will melt. You put your arms around them and think, "Am I crazy or what? I just love this person."

Then you think, "That has to be God because it would not be my first choice."

When you have gone through this training and have this kind of intimacy with Jesus, you feel His heart.

> **A true prophet will look at someone and see that small fleck of Jesus in them and try to bring it out.**

He will see their potential, their gifts, their ministry, their hunger and desire for the Lord - even if it is buried deep down inside.

Can you see why God has given you such a compassionate heart? Underneath all the fluff, He has given you tenderness, and there are times where you will cry for nothing.

It is His heart that He is trying to give you. Why do you keep despising this weakness? Why do you keep throwing away the one thing that makes you so precious?

This heart of yours is the one thing that is a priceless gift to the Church.

Prophetic Orientation vs. Prophetic Ministry

Starting out, you will come to the Lord with a broken heart of your own. It is this brokenness that drew you to Christ. From abusive experiences as a child to rejection from those you love, there is no lack of scarring in the heart of the prophet. When the Lord Jesus picks you up, you are broken and bleeding.

You are bruised, and while you do carry a heart to reach out to others just like yourself, you find yourself tripping over your own hurt. You are full of preconceived ideas and find yourself lashing out when you should love and being overly understanding when you should be firm.

Is it any surprise that you are in such a state? With so much hurt and so little healing, it is hard to navigate the waters of prophetic ministry effectively. That is why during the first season of your training, the Lord Jesus draws you into intimacy with Him. He begins peeling back the layers of your insecurity and fears and brings the balm of healing you crave so much.

You find your heart full and satisfied and for the first time in your life, you find someone that understands and is willing to go through with you. When I begin to think about why I am so faithful to Jesus, I need not go any further than that.

You see, He was there to heal my "ugly" when everyone just saw my hard edge and not the bleeding underneath it. When my flesh ran rampant, and I was screaming inside for someone to understand, He stood quietly next to me with His hand on my shoulder. When He found me, I was broken and the embodiment of self-pity and selfishness.

He reached out and reached the part of my heart that was buried under all of it and pulled out the small nugget of gold I had. He looked past my hard edge. Each time I ran to Him, He was right there. It was not a "once off event" but seasons upon seasons of laying in His arms and receiving the love my heart needed to heal.

When you have looked into His eyes for that long and become so saturated with His healing balm, it equips you in a way nothing else can. It equips you to heal others, because you have received that healing for yourself. You in turn, impart the very thing to others you craved since you were a young child.

Of all the signs, this one resonates deeply in the heart of anyone with a true prophetic call. Your journey has been long. The healing has, at times, been painful, but it is because of all this that you can say,

> *Isaiah 61:3* *To console those who mourn in Zion,*
> *To give them beauty for ashes,*
> *The oil of joy for mourning,*
> *The garment of praise for the spirit of heaviness;*
> *That they may be called trees of righteousness,*
> *The planting of the Lord, that He may be glorified."*

PROPHETIC ORIENTATION VS. PROPHETIC OFFICE

Chapter 07 – Prophetic Orientation vs. Prophetic Office

Sign #8 A Leader that Builds the Apostle's Pattern

> ***Ephesians 2:20*** *having been built on the foundation of the apostles and prophets, Jesus Christ Himself being the chief cornerstone,*

A prophet in office is a leader who builds the apostle's pattern. He works side by side with the apostle. It is the second highest ministry office. However, you would not say so looking at a lot of what we see today.

The prophet in office builds something that remains, something real and tangible. You are not going to build something real and tangible only giving prophetic words and revelation.

You are going to have to get your hands dirty and get into people's lives. You are going to have to identify their ministries, help them find their place, parent them, pastor them, and sometimes you may even need to be an evangelist just to get your point across.

However, because you are in prophetic office, you have already gone through all of that training. Like I shared before, you have gone through the body ministries.

You have been through the evangelistic or the pastoral ministries, depending on what your character was like, so that God could add that to you before you made your way to prophetic office.

So, you have everything that you need. You can counsel, although, you will do it prophetically. You can prophesy, and you can even preach and teach, prophetically.

You will do whatever you have to do. Yet, your purpose will never change, which is to help people find their place, bring them into a face-to-face relationship with Jesus, to equip the saints, to mature them, to train them, and to leave something that remains.

You are called to be a leader, and you are called to be a lot more than you realize.

Prophetic Orientation vs. Prophetic Office

> *Jeremiah 1:10 See, I have this day set you over the nations and over the kingdoms,*
> *To root out and to pull down,*
> *To destroy and to throw down,*
> *To build and to plant."*

This is a huge shift for someone who has only felt the first signs of their prophetic call to become someone who is appointed to office. Many prophets are thrust into seasons of loneliness during their training. Often because they or the pastor (or both) do not know how to handle this little fledgling prophet that tends to put their foot in it and rock the boat just after it got nice and calm!

Yeah, we can be pretty erratic in those early days (Don't pretend that you were all sugar and spice in the mouth of your pastor and apostle in the early days. You and I both know that there was a hint of bitterness and at times just a whole lot of chili pepper that sent everyone reeling!)

So what a shift it is when God takes the ugly duckling and then places him in a place to be actively involved in lives of others and to build a work that remains. I think that most prophets get the meaning in the book of Jeremiah where he is told he would "tear down" but many have yet to understand the concept of "building and planting"!

What do you think the point of all these seasons of fire is about? Do you think that the Lord spent all this time to make you into a vessel of honor, just to put you on the shelf? No! A vessel goes through the shaping it does, so that it might be used for a purpose.

Sure, while it is being shaped, it can do nothing but sit on the potter's wheel and get poked and prodded. You get pieces added and taken off and when it gets to a point of pain where you want to give up… you are put in the fire and baked solid!

There is a purpose to all of this. It is so that you might build and plant. You will soon come to understand that although the prophet is indeed called to also root out and pull down, the "rooting" and "pulling" begins in your own heart and mind as the Holy Spirit takes away more of "you" and so deposits more of Jesus.

So, look back. Where were you then? Where are you now? Just realizing your call? Are you on the potter's wheel? Are you through with the process? Well, once God is done, your work really begins. For then it is time to join the rest of the vessels and to play your part. In this case, it is in working with the apostle. For those wanting more on this, refer to *The Prophetic Mandate* where I flesh it out a bit more for you.

Sign #9 Introduces Church to the Realm of the Spirit

The prophet introduces the Church to the realm of the Spirit. You know how I said in *Today's Teacher* that the teacher has a hunger for the Word and that they show you the character of the Word?

Not only does the prophet show you the character of Jesus, but he opens up to you the realm of the Spirit. You cannot be in the presence of a prophet and not want to see visions or prophesy.

People think, "I am so jealous. I wish I could do that."

It is about time we start teaching God's people that they can do that, prophets. It is time we sit down and shut up and put some fire on everyone else to get out there and start prophesying.

Let the body minister to itself. Paul said:

> *Colossians 3:16 Let the word of Christ dwell in you richly in all wisdom, teaching and admonishing one another in psalms and hymns and spiritual songs, singing with grace in your hearts to the Lord.*

It did not say that the prophet has a hymn, a song, and a word. However, you would think that this is what the scripture says if you look at some churches.

My husband calls me a "papegaai". In Afrikaans that means, "parrot". I can just talk and talk like a parrot! But, sometimes we just need to shut up and teach God's people to rise up and let the Body minister to itself.

Imagine a church where they are all ministering to one another so effectively that we could step out and go to another church and get them to do that too.

Then, you are building something that remains. So yes, the prophet introduces the church to the realm of the Spirit so that they can minister to one another.

You see, after the prophet comes, the teachers start to come to life, the pastors start to come to life, and everyone starts to find their place.

Next thing you know, Joe in the corner is prophesying and Susie who sits in the back has a hymn, and no one knew she could even sing…

Is she a prophet? No. She just loves to sing. She loves Jesus.

We have a weird guy that likes to minister to old people, and he is the only one that likes to minister to old people, but when the prophet comes in, this guy finds a place.

Next thing you know, all the elderly in the church are happy. We are all meant to be ministering to each other, but we are so busy doing the work all by ourselves in the fivefold ministry that we forget that we are meant to be equipping the saints.

What are we going to do? Equip the saints to stand there and watch us?

No, they are meant to be doing all the ministry. Let's get our issues dealt with already. Let's get through the fire so that we can be equipped ourselves to be able to pour that out to the Church.

Prophetic Orientation vs. Prophetic Office

Huge shift for sure! Chances are that you started your ministry steps with a good dose of rejection. Ah yes, that mouth of yours that had so much good intention, but still managed to say it all wrong.

Good news! You do not stay that way forever. A time is coming when God will not only use that big mouth of yours, but you will train others as well!

From being rejected and pushed aside, doors will open, and people will come to receive from you. You will be as a mother who will bring her children and put them on her knee to instruct them. You will be as a father who reaches out in tenderness to show God's children how to enter into the Throne Room and experience Him for themselves.

Yes, prophet, it's true, a day is coming when you will be in high demand – not for the revelations that you can give, but for the person you are. You will gather many unto you, not because you are so "spiritual" but because you are the kind of person believers want to be around. People will want to receive what you have.

Sign #10 An Overcomer – Healed, Armed and Equipped

A prophet in office is also an overcomer. He can minister inner healing because he has been through it himself. That is how you are also going to recognize someone who is in office.

If you see a prophet calling themselves a prophet, and they are standing up and you look at them and see that they are very wounded and broken and have not had healing yet, then that is not someone that is in office.

I am not saying that prophets are a perfect work. There are deeper healings that God takes us through, even after office. However, if you are so broken and wounded that you can barely stand up, then you are not in office.

If you have been through the training, you know what I am talking about. God takes you through a season I illustrate from Elijah's "Zarephath" where one thing after the other comes up, and all the templates of the past, hurts, and rejection are put in your face.

Why is this? It is so that you can receive victory and healing. This way, you can be equipped to heal others. You cannot heal others when you are blubbering, bleeding, and crying all over them.

That is embarrassing. Let's stop that. We may start off wounded and broken, but that is why God calls us, to make sure we know what it feels like.

However, He wants us to go through the healing process so that we can then identify those that are broken and help them. He does not intend for you to stay broken and unarmed!

No, He intends for you to learn the lessons, become equipped and ready to be sent out.

> *2 Timothy 4:11* *Only Luke is with me. Get Mark and bring him with you, for he is useful to me for ministry.*

Look at what Paul says about Mark right here. Now this same Mark is the one and only that Paul and Barnabas had a fight over. Barnabas wanted to keep Mark with them, but Paul did not. Paul did not consider Mark mature enough to stay with them, because he caved under the pressure and deserted them when they needed him.

Prophetic Orientation vs. Prophetic Office

My, my, how times have changed. From Mark being at the center of a huge conflict, Paul now says "bring good old Mark along... he is useful to me now!"

That's you, prophet! Yes, you started out a bit wobbly on your feet and made a few mistakes, but you have gone through the process. You have learned spiritual warfare, how to minister, overcome your hurts from the past and learned to walk in a face-to-face relationship with Jesus.

You are useful to the apostle now. You are useful for the fivefold ministry now. You are useful to the body of Christ now.

Sign #11 A Mentor and Team Leader

Finally, the prophet is a mentor and a team leader. You are called to a leadership office. God has called you to be a model in His church. You are someone that others can look at and say, "I want to be like that. I want to model my life after someone like that."

When someone models themselves after you, they take on a lot more than what you say and prophesy. They pick up your spirit, your strengths, your anointing, your demons (OUCH... but true too), your hurt, your oppression, your sin, your laws of judgment, and your pride.

So, you better make sure that you have gone through the process and the fire. So, for someone who is in office, do you see why I say so often that to stand in office means to stand in fear and trembling?

You say, "Lord, I better be standing righteous before you because if I lay hands, if I prophesy, if it is contaminated, they are going to have curses manifest in their lives."

Isn't it so confusing when you see someone stand up and give a prophetic word and you know it is God because you sense God on it, but yet there is something that tags along with it?

You think, "Why did everything go wrong after this prophet came to our church? There were curses, people died, people got into car accidents...."

You know what I am talking about. This has happened in so many churches already.

"Why did this happen?" You ask, "Aren't they a prophet?"

I do not doubt that they are called, but have they gone through the fire? Have they dealt with their sin, their demons, and their open doors before they stood up and released that word?

We are called to be models. By the time you stand up, make sure that you have left the dross behind that needed to go.

I am not saying that we all suddenly reach a stage of perfection when we reach office. Hardly! I think that we only start to learn the real lessons when we are placed in office. It's only then that the true experience is forged after understanding everything in theory.

Do You Smell Like Smoke?

However, when you have been through the sanctification and training process, you do not come out of it unchanged. My uncle said something so appropriate to this point.

He said that often when he is around someone that has been through the fire we are talking about here, he smells smoke in the spirit. Then he knows that this is someone who has been in the fire for the call. He said to me, "When I am around you and Craig, I smell smoke!"

So, prophet, do you smell like smoke? You cannot remain in the fire for so long and remain unchanged. No one is that stubborn. Certainly not one with a fire to reach out and heal God's people.

Depending on how willing you have been to remain in that fire and go through the process, will depend on what percentage of you is gold and how much are impurities that still need to go.

As you go through training, a lot of those impurities are exposed. As you learn the ropes of spiritual warfare, you learn to deal with the sins of the heart that give satan license in your life. As you reach office, the process continues.

Prophetic Orientation vs. Prophetic Office

In South Africa, gold mining is a huge industry and you would think that gold would need to be put in the fire just once to be processed. However, this is untrue. The refining process takes time and also depends on how pure you want the gold to be.

What we call "dross" is actually a mixture of various different metals and rock that gets caught up in the gold when it is mined. No one wants nickel in their gold! And so the gold gets put into the fire time and again and each time that dross is scraped off, the gold becomes purer.

Each sin, preconceived idea, and hurt are strains of impure metals that the Holy Spirit has worked on during this process.

Each strain of nickel and rock has been replaced with more of Christ. He has given you beauty for ashes. He has given you a sword for your hurt and a shield for your failure. He has replaced the carnal flesh in you for the balm of healing and power of the Spirit.

When you have gone through this process, you are equipped with the tools to train others. You identify their impurities. You see their demons. You identify their hurts. Yes, the Lord gives you spiritual revelation, but let's get a little real here. When you have "been through", it does not take much to see that same hurt in the eyes of others.

Come now, for those who have dealt with demons, when you see that same demon attacking someone else, you see it from a mile away. You know its voice – you know how it feels. You do not need to try hard to see what you are up against!

You are suddenly someone else's hope. Now, prophet, I know that you have navigated much of this on your own. Who was there for you when the voice of accusation and the slimy touch of deception and divination was crawling all over you?

Many times, it felt like you had to pull yourself up by your own bootstraps. You fought the devil in hand-to-hand combat at times. You cried alone at night when the bills could not be paid, and you rocked yourself to sleep when your marriage felt like it would never recover.

Only you and Jesus knew exactly how much those words of rejection hurt. Who was there for you? Prophet, Jesus was always there for you, and each time He picked you up, He healed you. He gave you something new.

And now… well, now you can make sure that no one else has to face what you did. They do not need to be alone. The broken children of God do not have to go to sleep alone at night without anyone to show them the way.

When they are broken, you have an answer of healing. When they are rejected, you have just the right word. When their marriage is crushed, you know how to do warfare and to pick up that broken couple from the battlefield. You are there to patch them up, put a fire in them, and send them out again.

They never need to be alone again, because they have you. Isn't this the point? In a church with so many prophets, can some at least stop for long enough to make sure that others do not need to go through the same trials that we did?

What is the purpose otherwise? What was the point of going on this journey if it was not to make sure that others do not need to?

God has called you to do so much more than just overcome your hurt, He has called you to be an example and leader to make sure that His people always have someone to come to with theirs.

Will you be that person? Are you all the way through? Have you taken your time out in the fire? Have you taken the time to be healed and equipped? If so, then you are ready prophet. You are ready to stand in office and be the one still standing after the enemy has shot his biggest shot!

THE WEIGHT OF THE CHURCH

Chapter 08 – The Weight of the Church

Now after going through all those signs, I am pretty sure that you got the concept that prophetic orientation and prophetic office are not the same thing. There are many who will go into prophetic ministry, and many who will flow in the gifts of the spirit.

However, if you want to stand in prophetic office, I want you to feel the weight of the Church. It is like Paul said, "I have been beaten, I have been shipwrecked, I have lost everything, and I nearly died a couple times, but nothing compares to the weight of the Church." (2 Corinthians 11:22-28)

I am putting that weight on you. I want you to feel how responsible you are for the Church. God holds you responsible. To whom much is given, much is also required.

A new believer will sin, and you will sin and God will come down on you and not them. Why is this? Why does God come down on you?

It is for the same reason that He would come down on the shepherds that lead the sheep astray. It is because He has given you that responsibility and authority. Use it wisely.

Stand in it boldly and know above all of this, whether you fail or succeed (you will do both), He will finish what He has started in you. At the end of the day, it is the Holy Spirit that will take you through the training.

It is the Lord Jesus that puts you in office and even once you are there, He is the one who continues to mature you in your call and causes those gifts to manifest again and again.

If you can get that one principle, it will bring a peace to your training. He is in control. Just listen for the cues.

Identify when He is killing your flesh, identify when He is resurrecting you, and identify when He is saying, "not here" and "not now".

Submit to His hand because when you do that, you will become the prophet that the Church sorely needs.

Isn't it sad that we have a Church that does not know Jesus? I have been to so many kinds of churches, Pentecostal, Baptist, Methodist, Non-denominational and "prophetic". I have seen so many people standing up and crying out to God asking for Him to manifest Himself.

They worship and cry out to the Lord as if they need to twist His arm to make an appearance.

I am like, "Guys, He is right here. Can you not see Him?"

They are following one church trend after the other, trying to find Jesus. Some run after Israel and the Jewish culture. They think, "If I perform this right or celebrate this holiday, then God will bless me."

They strive and strive. They say, "Let me fast, pray, and give money to the church and then God will be happy with me."

I just want to die inside when I see this. I say, "Jesus, they do not know you, do they?"

They know the fire of the Holy Spirit and the judgment of sin of the Father, but when is the Church going to fall in love with Jesus?

When are they going to realize that He accepts them regardless and that He wants to change them and that He is there at their lowest time? When are they going to know how much He adores them and how beautifully made they are?

When will they see how much He wants to heal them and that it was not Him that did those things to them? They need to stop trying to prove themselves and just climb onto His knee and fall like a child onto His lap and into His arms.

You know this love, but we forget sometimes how powerful the soaking love and acceptance of Jesus is. Like an underground stream that waters the ground from deep within until it is saturated. It washes away the years of famine and drenches the dry, cold recesses of our hearts.

His love crumbles the heart of stone and melts the ice we surround ourselves with. Of all the ministry we can offer, is presenting the love of Jesus as a force not the greatest? To minister in the love anointing and allow God's people to just sit in it and allow it to wash over them a while?

That is all He made us for. He made us to love Him. He does not want our prayers, our sacrifices, our circumcision, or any of that. He wants our hearts, our love.

When is the Church going to get the message? They are going to get the message when you get the message.

Put away your striving, your prophecies, your titles, and put away all of "you" and then, put on Christ. Stand in the image of Christ in the reality of your brokenness, but in the power of His grace.

Then, you and I will build an End-Times Church. We are going to build something that remains and that will stay from generation to generation.

About the Author

Born in Bulawayo, Zimbabwe and raised in South Africa, Colette had a zeal to serve the Lord from a young age. Coming from a long line of Christian leaders and having grown up as a pastor's kid, she is no stranger to the realities of ministry. Despite having to endure many hardships such as her parent's divorce, rejection, and poverty, she continues to follow after the Lord passionately. Overcoming these obstacles early in her life has built a foundation of compassion and desire to help others gain victory in their lives.

Since then, the Lord has led Colette, with her husband, Craig Toach, to establish *Apostolic Movement International,* a ministry to train and minister to Christian leaders all over the world, where they share all the wisdom that the Lord has given them through each and every time they chose to walk through the refining fire in their personal lives, as well as in ministry.

In addition, Colette is a fantastic cook, an amazing mom to not only her 4 natural children, but to her numerous spiritual children all over the world. Colette is also a renowned author, mentor, trainer and a woman that has great taste in shoes! The scripture to "be all things to all men" definitely applies here, and the Lord keeps adding to that list of things each and every day.

How does she do it all? Experience through every book and teaching the life of an apostle firsthand, and get the insight into how the call of God can make every aspect of your life an incredible adventure.

Read more at www.colette-toach.com

Connect with Colette Toach on Facebook!
www.facebook.com/ColetteToach

Check Colette out on Amazon.com at:
www.amazon.com/author/colettetoach

Recommendations by the Author

Note: All reference of AMI refers to Apostolic Movement International.

If you enjoyed this book, I know you will also love the following books and recommendations.

The Fivefold Office Series

By Colette Toach

The Fivefold Offices for Today (Book 1)

Are you an Apostle, Prophet, Teacher, Pastor, or Evangelist? Are you called to walk the social, business, or ministry road? It is time to reveal the road ahead of you, and to rise up into the fullness of your call.

Today's Evangelist (Book 2)

In this book, Colette Toach will show you where the evangelist came from, what their role is in the fivefold ministry, and how and where they operate. So be prepared to go higher and understand your call as an evangelist like never before.

Today's Pastor (Book 3)

Perhaps you have felt that pull already, the pull of those sheep coming to you for help, and sharing things they really shouldn't, because they feel you will be able to help them. Welcome to being a pastor! It is time to discover what that truly means.

Today's Teacher (Book 4)

As a teacher, God is calling you to change mindsets, build solid foundations, and shake up old ones. You have been called to equip the body of Christ with the sword of the Lord that will never grow dull and give the tools that are needed to start a reformation.

Prophetic Mandate

By Colette Toach

Colette Toach gives you all the details, insight and practical how-tos of what the Lord gives each and every prophet once they reach office: a mandate. Do not let the price you have paid go to waste. Walk out your calling with all the power, anointing and authority the Lord has given you!

The Prophetic Field Guide Series

By Colette Toach

Prophetic Essentials

If it burns in you to pay any price that is necessary and to stand up and break down the barriers between the Lord Jesus and His Bride, then my friend, you have picked up the right tool that will confirm the call of God on your life.

Prophetic Functions

There is so much more to the prophet than standing up in church and prophesying. Be prepared to live and experience the Lord like never before. This is not fiction... this is your training guide to the prophetic.

Prophetic Anointing

God has promised you a visit to the throne room! This is your summons from Almighty God. It is time for you to experience Him face-to-face and heart-to-heart. Get ready for the meeting of a lifetime. It is time to flow in the anointing in ways you never knew were possible.

Prophetic Boot Camp

So, prophet of God, are you ready to sign up for boot camp? The Holy Spirit will be your sergeant and this book will be your training manual! Together you will be shaped, challenged, inspired and in the end, equipped to stand as a prophet in office.

Prophetic Warrior

Now is the time to get armed and to fulfill your function as a prophetic warrior. There is a reason you have a fire to storm the gates of hell. Consider this book your faithful navigator and secret doorway to engage in a new level of spiritual warfare.

Prophetic Counter Insurgence

Learn all about the "prophetic super spy", discover strategies that can be used in spiritual warfare, receive stealth training, find the secrets to dealing with fear of the mind, and where spiritual warfare begins and ends.

Prophetic Key

With each page, you will feel the weight of the Church being put on your shoulders. Up until now, it has been about your calling as a prophet, but from this point on, you will come to a newfound reality that this is about the calling of the Church, to the world.

Earn a Diploma That Truly Validates Your Call

With over twenty years' experience in full-time ministry, Apostles Craig and Colette Toach know the fire that burns in you, to do the work of God.

With a focus on spiritual parenting, mentorship and hands-on training, each school equips you to do the work of God. Consider us boot camp for your fivefold ministry call.

Each course is video based with required report submissions for you to complete after each lesson. Each student is allocated a trainer that marks all reports, follows up with personal ministry and laying on of hands at graduation.

AMI Prophetic School: www.prophetic-school.com

There is a clear track that the Holy Spirit follows to train up His prophets. Having trained prophets into office all over the world, your calling will find itself in an environment where your prophetic mandate is as important to us as it is to you.

Think: training, impartation and mentorship. By the time you walk the stage at your graduation, you would have done more than just studied for a diploma – you would have embarked on a journey that would have equipped you to fulfill your mandate as a prophet in office. www.prophetic-school.com

Pastor Teacher School:

www.pastorteacherschool.com

Everything you wish you knew about doing the work of the ministry. Our student complement exists of pastors, ministry leaders, apostles and various fivefold ministers who crave a deeper reality of the Lord and their calling.

With an emphasis on becoming equipped, each course gears you towards functioning in a leadership capacity. Whether that is behind the pulpit or in a home church setting, you will receive training that once you walk the stage would already be gearing you towards apostolic ministry. www.pastorteacherschool.com

AMI Campus: www.ami-campus.com

Not ready to commit to a lengthy training program? No problem! You are welcome to study independently and pick and choose between prophetic, pastoral, teaching and apostolic courses that tailor fit you right where you are at.

The main difference between our public campus and our other schools is that associates in our campus are not allocated a specific trainer, but all projects are marked by our full trainer complement. This option is perfect for those who are self-disciplined and know exactly where God is taking them.

NOTE: Courses completed in campus qualify for a certificate of completion, but do not qualify towards credits for a diploma or graduation. www.ami-campus.com

Contact Information

To check out our wide selection of materials, go to:
www.ami-bookshop.com

Do you have any questions about any products?

Contact us at: +1 (760) 466 - 7679
(9am to 5pm California Time, Weekdays Only)

E-mail Address: admin@ami-bookshop.com

Postal Address:

>A.M.I.
>5663 Balboa Ave #416
>San Diego, CA 92111, USA

Facebook Page:
http://www.facebook.com/ApostolicMovementInternational

YouTube Page:
https://www.youtube.com/c/ApostolicMovementInternational

Twitter Page: https://twitter.com/apmoveint

Amazon.com Page: www.amazon.com/author/colettetoach

AMI Bookshop
It's not **Just Knowledge**, It's **Living Knowledge**

Made in the USA
Coppell, TX
16 January 2021